BET YOU CAN'T!

This fascinating book, chock-full of entertaining tricks to try out on family and friends, proves that science can be fun. Each one is designed to tempt your victim into trying something impossible. And at the same time you'll be learning how basic principles of science ensure you can't lose the bets.

The tricks are grouped according to the principles they use: gravity and balance, mechanics (force and motion), fluids (gases and liquids), mathematics (without numbers), energy and perception. The authors explain simply and vividly how these principles apply in each case, whether it be trying to blow up a balloon in a bottle or to lift someone by the elbows. So not only is *Bet You Can't!* a source of hours of entertainment, it is also a valuable introduction to a variety of important scientific concepts.

Vicki Cobb was born in New York City, USA, and has written many science-related books for young readers, as well as creating and hosting a television show called *The Science Game*. Born in New York state, Kathy Darling has written and edited children's books and has worked as a columnist and publisher. *Bet You Can't!* was winner of the New York Academy of Science's Children's Science Book Award.

VICKI COBB AND KATHY DARLING

BET YOU CAN'T!

SCIENCE IMPOSSIBILITIES
TO FOOL YOU

Illustrated by Martha Weston

Puffin Books

PUFFIN BOOKS

Published by the Penguin Group
Penguin Books Ltd, 27 Wrights Lane, London W8 5TZ, England
Penguin Books USA Inc., 375 Hudson Street, New York, New York 10014, USA
Penguin Books Australia Ltd, Ringwood, Victoria, Australia
Penguin Books Canada Ltd, 10 Alcorn Avenue, Toronto, Ontario, Canada M4V 3B2
Penguin Books (NZ) Ltd, 182–190 Wairau Road, Auckland 10, New Zealand

Penguin Books Ltd, Registered Offices: Harmondsworth, Middlesex, England

First published in the USA by Avon Books 1980
This edition published in Puffin Books 1988
3 5 7 9 10 8 6 4

Copyright © Vicki Cobb and Kathy Darling, 1980
All rights reserved

Printed in England by Clays Ltd, St Ives plc
Set in 11/13pt Monophoto Photina

Except in the United States of America, this book is sold subject
to the condition that it shall not, by way of trade or otherwise, be lent,
re-sold, hired out, or otherwise circulated without the publisher's
prior consent in any form of binding or cover other than that in
which it is published and without a similar condition including this
condition being imposed on the subsequent purchaser

Dedicated to P. T. Barnum,
who also believed that there is
a sucker born every minute

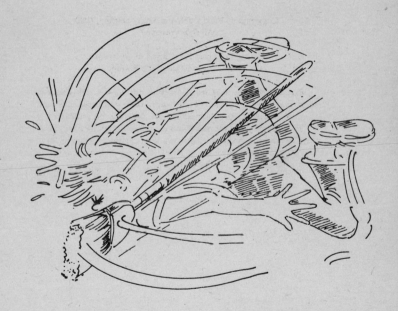

CONTENTS

THE SURE THING

Bet you can't read this book without trying at least one trick. They look s-o-o-o easy, you won't be able to resist. But anyone who takes these bets is in for a truly humbling experience, for this is a collection of sucker bets. There is no way to win. Each challenge is designed to trick you into trying something impossible.

These really are impossible tricks. If at first you don't succeed . . . perhaps you never will. Not all things are possible. It takes a wise person properly to assess a losing situation and walk away from futility. Contrary to what you may have heard, failing is no disgrace.

But, deep inside, everybody wants to be a winner. Now you *can* be. Just use this book. The bets are all fixed. Every time you will be a sure-fire, guaranteed, perpetual winner. Fool your friends, amaze your parents, and outsmart your teachers. Won't it be nice to have the odds stacked in your favour for a change?

Actually the odds were stacked at the beginning of time by Mother Nature. It took some of the greatest minds in the history of the world to figure out what was happening. Galileo, Newton and a number of others saw beyond the limits of human senses and experiences. They reasoned and experimented and figured out why some things just won't work. Now you can cash in on their discoveries.

Take a chance. Even if the odds are insurmountable, you're bound to have a good time. *We'll* bet on that!

1

THE ARTFUL USE OF GRAVITY

Gravity is the biggest downer of all time. True? Yes. But, surprise! Gravity can pull sideways or even up. The sun is pulling on the earth in a direction that is anything but down.

Gravity is the force of attraction between two masses, and when it's the only force operating, it draws the smaller mass to the larger one. The reason we think of gravity as a downer is because the most familiar example is the force of attraction between the giant earth and our body.

One way gravity exerts its force is very curious. All the weight of a body seems to be concentrated at a single centre point. If a body has a supporting base, its 'centre of gravity' must be located directly over the base or the body will tip over. When an object has a regular shape, like the earth, it is easy to locate the centre of gravity because it is at the geometric centre. A see-saw is balanced at its geometric centre, its centre of gravity.

But irregularly shaped objects, like the human body, do not have a centre of gravity that necessarily coincides with the geometric centre. In fact, the centre of gravity can be moved around. Skiing, for example, is one sport where an athlete is constantly shifting his or her centre of gravity to maintain balance. In this chapter, you may be moving your centre of gravity

around. That's where the fun comes in. The artful use of gravity can throw you totally off balance. Want a bet?

UP AGAINST THE WALL

BET YOU CAN'T PICK UP A BANKNOTE THAT'S RIGHT IN FRONT OF YOU!

The Set-up: Stand with your heels against a wall and your feet together. Place a banknote on the floor about 30 centimetres in front of your feet. Now . . . try to pick up the note without moving your feet or bending your knees.

The Trick: That note is as safe as if it were in the bank. You can't pick it up. Here's why. When you stand straight against the wall, your centre of gravity is over your feet (base), as it should be. When you bend forwards, you move your centre of gravity forwards. In order to keep your balance, you must move your feet forwards too. This maintains the base under the centre of gravity needed for stability. Since the rules of this trick don't allow you to move your feet, you're noteless. And if you persist in trying to pick it up, you'll fall flat on your face!

While you are standing there with your back to the wall, here are some more wasted efforts.

BET YOU CAN'T JUMP!

The Set-up: Keep your heels, hips and shoulders against the wall. Without leaning forwards, try to jump. What's the matter? Are your feet stuck to the floor?

BET YOU CAN'T LIFT YOUR FOOT OFF THE FLOOR!

The Set-up: Turn your right side to the wall. Put your right foot and cheek against the wall. Now try to lift your left foot off the floor.

The Trick: Both of these stunts require you to shift your

centre of gravity away from the support base. The first can't be done without falling over, and the second can't be done without moving the wall. The body maintains balance with little adjustments so automatic that we never think about them.

SEX-LINKED BEHAVIOUR

BET YOU CAN'T PICK UP A CHAIR UNLESS YOU ARE FEMALE!

The Set-up: Here's something your mother can do but your father can't. Begin by having the subject back away from a wall to a distance of four foot-lengths. Place a chair or stool between the person and the wall. Instruct the person to lean over and rest his or her forehead against the wall. Now the subject must pick up the chair and try to straighten up without touching the chair to the wall.

The Trick: The reason men can't do this trick is because

15

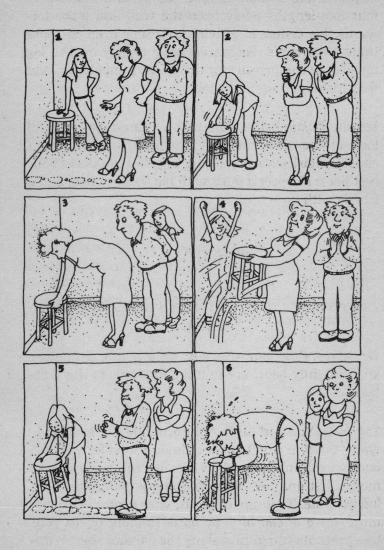

they have big feet! Women have feet that are smaller in proportion to their height. So, when a man backs four foot-lengths away from the wall and leans forwards, his centre of gravity is further from his base than a woman's. He would have to rely on the leg muscles to compensate for this greater imbalance, and they just aren't up to the job.

Possible Pitfall: Before you do this stunt, take a careful look at the shoes of your potential subjects. Don't choose a girl who is wearing big, heavy boots. Your best bet is to select a male with big, heavy boots and a female with high heels.

TOE HOLD

BET YOU CAN'T JUMP FORWARDS ON YOUR TOES!

The Set-up: Hold your toes with your hands. Keep your knees slightly bent. Try to jump forwards in this position.

The Trick: You can jump right around the block backwards but you won't get one single bound forwards. A backward jump is possible because the support base moves first and the centre of gravity maintains a balanced state. To jump forwards, your centre of gravity must move ahead of your base. Holding on to your toes prevents you from making the balance shift. Without shifting your centre of gravity, your leg muscles would have to be strong enough not only to lift your body off the ground but also to support the unbalanced position you would be in while jumping. We've heard that football players have such strength in their leg muscles, but we've yet to find someone who can do this stunt.

GLUED TO YOUR CHAIR?

**BET YOU CAN'T GET UP FROM A CHAIR!
NO GIMMICKS! NO STRINGS EITHER!**

The Set-up: All you have to do to win is get up from a chair. Sit in a straight-backed armless chair. Keep your back against the back of the chair and put your feet flat on the floor. Fold your arms across your chest.

18

Now, keeping your feet flat and your back straight, try to stand up.

The Trick: We lied about the gimmick. The gimmick is gravity. In the sitting position the centre of gravity is at the base of your spine. By trying to stand up with your back straight, you prevent the centre of gravity from moving to a position above the feet, which are your support base. Human thigh muscles simply aren't strong enough to compensate for the balance problems during the getting-up period. So you remain glued to your chair.

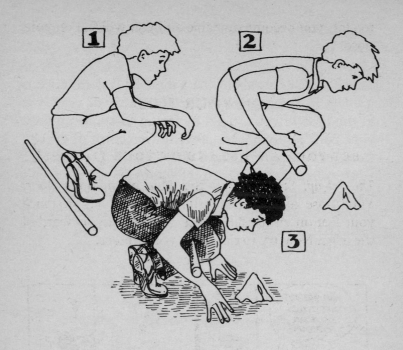

NOSEDIVE

BET YOU CAN'T PICK UP A HANDKERCHIEF WITH YOUR TEETH!

The Set-up: Squat down. Place a broom handle under your bent knees and crook your elbows around it. Now put a handkerchief on the ground in front of you. Lean forwards, using your hands for balance, and try to pick up the handkerchief with your teeth.

The Trick: As you rotate forwards towards the handkerchief, the centre of gravity is shifting away from the stable position directly above your feet. Once it goes too far, you become unstable and you will fall on your nose.

ON YOUR TOES

BET YOU CAN'T STAND ON YOUR TIPTOES!

The Set-up: Stand facing the edge of an open door. Your nose and stomach should just touch it. Place your feet on either side of the door slightly forward of the edge. Now try to rise on to your tiptoes.

The Trick: You'll be caught flat-footed on this one. The reason you can't do this trick is because it moves your base of support out from under your centre of gravity. In order to stand on your toes, you must transfer the

centre of gravity forwards. To transfer the centre forwards, you must lean over. The door prevents you
from doing this.

AN UNBEATABLE FAST BALL

BET YOU CAN'T BEAT ME IN A ROLLING CONTEST!

The Set-up: This rolling contest has three participants.
Each person chooses an object to roll from one of these
groups:

> spheres: marbles, golf balls, ball-bearings (be sure they
> are solid balls, not hollow like a Ping-Pong ball);

discs: draughts, plastic plates, coasters;
hoops: rings, tyres, hula hoops.

The contest must take place on an incline. Choose a slanted board or a smooth, sloping driveway depending on the size of the objects chosen. At a signal, let all three objects roll towards a finishing line.

The Trick: No one will beat you if you choose your object from the group of spheres. All spheres will beat all discs, which will beat all hoops. We mean ALL. It doesn't matter how heavy or how big the objects are. Rolling speed is directly related to the distribution of weight around an object's centre of gravity, known as its 'moment of inertia'. In all three kinds of objects, the centre of gravity is the geometric centre. But the weights are distributed differently.

In the case of the hoop, all the weight is located

away from the centre of gravity. Of the three types of objects, it has the largest moment of inertia. The solid ball has the smallest since its weight is most closely distributed around its centre of gravity. The closer the mass or weight of an object is to its centre of gravity, the smaller its moment of inertia and the faster it can rotate.

You've seen this principle at work as an ice skater goes into a spin. The spin begins with the arms extended. As the spin progresses, the arms are drawn towards the body, decreasing the moment of inertia by bringing the weight closer to the centre, and thus increasing the velocity of the spin.

STRONG WORDS

BET YOU CAN'T OUTPULL A BOOK

The Set-up: Open a big, heavy book and place it face down in the centre of a 1.5-metre cord. Tie the cord in a knot along the spine. Grip one end of the cord in each hand at least half a metre away from the book. Now pull and try to bring the cord into a perfectly horizontal position with the knot in the centre.

The Trick: The cord will come close to horizontal, but it will never straighten out. That's because your muscle power is not equal to the force of gravity pulling on the book. When the cord is in a vertical position over the book, the force you need to exert to prevent the book from falling is equal to the weight of the book.

But as you move your hands apart, your muscle strength is delivered at an angle. Force delivered at an angle must be greater than the weight it is countering. The smaller the angle, the greater the force required. The closer you pull the cord to the horizontal position, the more strength you need to exert. The cord will snap before you level off.

This is really a tug of war between you and gravity. Gravity is a hands-down winner. But don't take our word for it. Try it yourself.

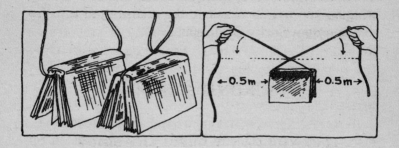

2

FORCES OF DECEPTION

Karate experts use science to defend themselves. Long before reaching the black-belt rank, they discover that mechanics, which is the branch of science dealing with forces and motion, is their most important defensive weapon.

Forces can be as invisible as gravity or pressure. Or they can be as impossible to ignore as a karate chop! But regardless of whether it is in the form of a push, pull, or collision, force can be made to work *for* you instead of *against* you.

In karate, force is never met head-on. Instead it is cleverly diverted or even turned back against an opponent. Some of the most spectacular and skilful moves often require little strength. They are tricky manipulations of force.

When forces meet head-on, if they are equal and in opposite directions, they cancel each other out and nothing happens. Two equal teams in a tug of war, for example, will often result in a stalemate. But unequal forces coming from *different* directions *can* affect an object. That's the secret of most martial arts. The angle of attack throws an opponent off balance when it comes from an unexpected direction.

This chapter does not deal with self-defence, but a lot of the secrets that karate, judo, and ju-jitsu students learn are used here. Tricks based on mechanical princi-

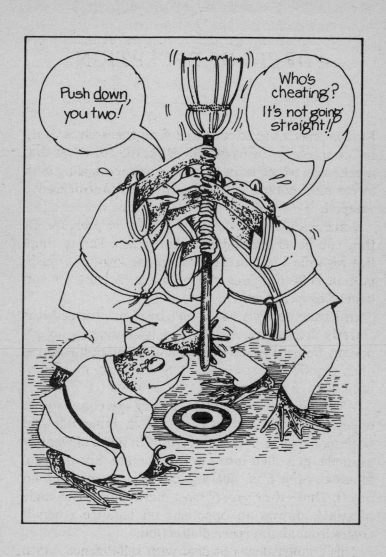

ples will give you some surprise moves, too. The only one you won't fool is Mother Nature!

A PRESSING PROBLEM

BET YOU CAN'T KEEP YOUR FISTS TOGETHER!

The Set-up: Here is the perfect trick to try on someone who is stronger than you. Ask the strong person to stand with arms extended, one fist on top of the other. To win, the strong person must keep the fists in this position as you try to separate them.

The Trick: This is child's play. It is so easy to separate the fists, you only need to use your index fingers. With a quick strike, push sideways on the back of each fist. They should move apart easily. (If the trick doesn't go as planned, check to see that the strong person isn't cheating by locking the lower thumb inside the upper fist.)

The strangest thing about this trick is that the harder the strong person tries to press the fists together, the easier it is for you to separate them. So urge your opponent to try harder!

In an effort to keep the fists together, the strong person concentrates all of his or her force in an up-and-down direction. Almost no strength is exerted sideways, which is where your attack comes from. Again, your independent force is in a different direction from your opponent's. That's why it is effective.

In addition, the fully extended arm cannot deliver nearly as much strength as a bent arm. The force in a fully extended arm comes from the shoulder. In a bent arm, the force to the fist comes from the elbow, a much shorter distance. This principle plays a larger role in the next trick.

A MATCH THAT'S NO CONTEST

The Set-up: Place a wooden match across the back of your middle finger and under the first and third fingers at the joints nearest the fingertips. Try to break the match by pressing up with the middle finger and down with the two others. Can't do it? Try pressing down with the middle finger and up with the other two. Don't let the thumb and little finger help out. That's considered cheating.

The Trick: This is an impossible situation because you are not using your fingers to gain a mechanical advantage. Your fingers can be used as levers, which are devices that can increase a force when used properly. The key to a lever is the location of the *fulcrum*, or point of attachment, and the force being delivered to it. When the force is close to the fulcrum, the force is increased. Thus, a crowbar can easily remove a nail from wood. But when the force is a distance from the fulcrum, it is weaker.

In this trick, the fulcrum is the set of knuckles where your fingers attach to your hand. When you try to deliver a force far from this point of attachment, your muscles are too weak to do the job. But move the match to the other side of the middle joints close to the knuckles and see how easily you can break it. Now your lever fingers can supply enough power.

LOWER THE BROOM

The Set-up: You will need four people, a big paper plate, and a broom. Put the paper plate on the floor. This is the target. Ask three people to hold a broom upside-down about half a metre above the target. They should hold the handle close to the bristle end. When they are in position, place your palm against the broom handle near the end. You may have to lie on the floor to do this. Now challenge the others to touch the broom to the target. As they try to push the broom down, you push sideways . . .

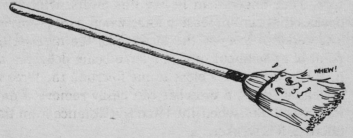

The Trick: This is an example of forces working independently of each other. The sideways force you exert is independent of the downward force of the

31

broom handle. Since you aren't opposing the down-ward force, you can easily deflect the broom handle away from the target with a smaller sideways force. So it doesn't matter how hard your three opponents push towards the ground, you can always prevent the broom from reaching the target.

NO PUSH-OVER

BET YOU CAN'T PUSH ME BACKWARDS!

The Set-up: Hold a broom handle horizontally in front of you. Extend your arms with your hands gripping the stick about the same distance apart as your shoulders. Challenge someone to try to push you backwards. He or she must grasp the middle of the stick and push using a steady, forward pressure (no sudden thrusts).

The Trick: It's impossible to move you a single inch backwards. The secret defence is force diversion, where-by you change the direction of your opponent's force. To do this, bend your elbows out like wings and push slightly upwards to counter any pressure. The force that is supposed to knock you backwards is diverted into your arms and upwards.

Possible Pitfall: This trick depends on timing, so you may need to practise it to make your moves at just the right moment.

While you have the broom handle and a friend, try this one too.

The Set-up: Hold the broom handle horizontally again, this time with your thumbs up, about 15 centimetres on either side of the centre of the stick. Ask your friend

to hold the ends of the stick and try to knock you off balance.

The Trick: When your opponent pushes forwards, you push the broom handle upwards. The force of the push will be deflected away from any direction that could knock you off balance. Hands on the centre of the stick. Hands on the ends of the stick. It doesn't matter. You can win either way.

AN UNTEARABLE SITUATION

BET YOU CAN'T RIP A TISSUE!

The Set-up: You will need a paper tissue, a cardboard tube from a roll of paper towels, a rubber band, table salt or sand, and a broom handle. Stretch the tissue across the end of the paper-towel tube. Fasten it in place with the rubber band. Pour 8 centimetres of salt or sand into the tube. Now hold the tube in one hand and jam a broom handle into the salt. Try to push hard enough to rip the tissue.

The Trick: The tissue is thin and the broom handle is strong, but you won't be able to rip that tissue! The force you put on the broom handle is not all going straight down the tube towards the tissue. There are many tiny spaces between the salt crystals. When you jam the broom handle into the salt, the crystals collide, sending the force in every direction. Salt absorbs some of the force and divides the rest so it is diverted to all

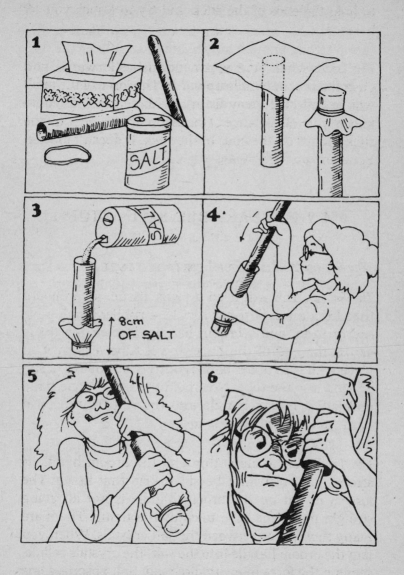

the surfaces of the tube. Only a tiny fraction of the original force reaches the tissue. The human body is not a strong enough power-house to deliver the force needed to send the broom handle through the tissue.

For centuries, bags of sand were used to stop speeding bullets in a dramatic adaptation of this marvel of nature.

A SURE RIP-OFF

BET YOU CAN'T TEAR A PIECE OF PAPER INTO THREE PIECES!

The Set-up: Fold a piece of paper into thirds. Open it out again. Now cut or tear the paper equally along the folds so that only about 2.5 centimetres of paper keeps the strips together. Hold the tops of the two end strips. Now try to tear the paper so that the middle strip drops out and there are three separate pieces of paper.

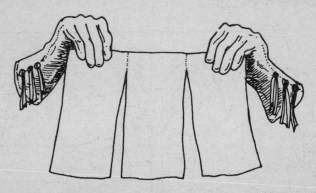

The Trick: Your strength here is weakness. Paper, like all other materials, succumbs to force at its weakest point. The two tears you started in the paper are weak points, and they are not equal even if they appear to be. There is no way you can make the cuts perfectly equal. When you pull, the weaker tear gives way first. This makes that spot even weaker, so any more force will be delivered directly to that point, until it rips completely off. Then you are left without the opposing force needed to separate the other two strips of paper.

NOTHING TO GET TORN UP ABOUT

BET YOU CAN'T MAKE TWO STRAIGHT TEARS IN A PAPER TOWEL!

The Set-up: The tears in this trick must be made at right angles to each other. Take a single sheet of paper towelling. Try to rip it in a straight line from one side to the other. If you succeed, then make a second tear from top to bottom.

The Trick: You can't make perpendicular straight-line

tears because paper towelling is formed on a wire screen, which creates straight lines in one direction. This is called the grain. The other direction does not have these unbroken parallel lines.

A force always attacks the weakest point. The parallel lines of the grain are thinner than the rest of the paper. So when you tear with the grain, the rip runs down one of the lines made by the wire and you get a straight edge. When you try to tear across the grain, the force attacks whatever point is weakest and a jagged, irregular line is produced.

ELBOWED OUT

BET YOU CAN'T BE LIFTED BY THE ELBOWS!

The Set-up: Stand upright with your elbows bent and held horizontally to your body. Rest your palms on your shoulders. Ask two strong people to hold your elbows (one apiece) and try to lift you off the ground.

The Trick: Your elbow angle is the difference between success and failure in this trick. The positioning of the elbows forward of the centre of gravity is what makes the elbow lift impossible. (Move your elbows back against your body, and you can be lifted easily.)

The elbows in front of your body move the applied lift force away from your centre of gravity. The more you increase this distance, the more force is needed to overcome the resistance of your weight. It's truly amaz-

ing how such a small distance puts this trick outside the realm of human strength.

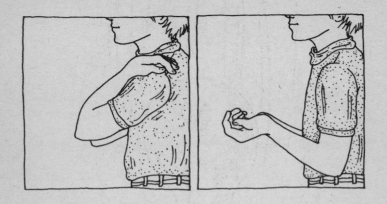

NO SHATTERING EXPERIENCE

BET YOU CAN'T BREAK A LIGHT BULB ON A CONCRETE FLOOR!

The Set-up: Check with an adult before doing this trick. Hold a burnt out light bulb over a concrete floor. The metal end must be facing straight down. If you think you can break the bulb on the floor, drop it! Yes, drop it.

The Trick: The bulb won't break. The reason is that the force of impact is absorbed by the metal part of the

bulb, which is practically unbreakable. The glass, which *can* shatter when force is applied, is protected by the metal base. Although the bulb may bounce around on the floor, these little bounces will not be enough to break the glass.

Caution: Do not *throw* the bulb at the floor. This may result in the bulb's hitting somewhere other than the metal end and the glass might shatter. For safety's sake, do not throw the bulb, just drop it.

A RAW DEAL

BET YOU CAN'T FOOL ME WITH A HARD-BOILED EGG!

The Set-up: You are the expert egg sorter in this trick. You will need a raw egg and a hard-boiled one. Without cracking either, you can identify the hard-boiled one just by spinning the eggs.

The Trick: Hard-boiled eggs spin faster and longer than raw eggs. A hard-boiled egg is a solid. It spins easily. A raw egg contains a liquid. Liquid requires more force than a solid to set it in motion. Since you apply one force to the egg when you spin it, the liquid inside the raw egg does not move as rapidly as the solid shell. This creates a drag between the inside of the shell and the surface of the liquid, which slows down and eventually stops the movement of the egg.

42

A PIERCING MOMENT

BET YOU CAN'T POP A BALLOON WITH A PIN!

The Set-up: Inflate and tie a balloon. Put a small piece of Sellotape on it. Now try to pop the balloon by sticking a pin through the tape. Be careful with the pin.

The Trick: The balloon is unpoppable! Air leaks out, but it won't deflate with a bang. Rubber and tape react differently to the stress created by the escaping air. The balloon skin is weak and rips when the air pushes against the edges of the hole. The tape is a stronger material and can resist the force of the compressed air.

An unpoppable balloon is a good party stunt, but can you see how this principle is used to make blow-out-proof tyres?

3

FLUID FOOLERS

Which of these are fluids: treacle, air, glass? (Hint: A fluid is anything that will flow unless it is restrained by a container.) If you answered all three, you're right. But you probably didn't guess correctly, because glass is a fluid fooler.

In most ways, glass is like a solid. You could call it a fluid, though, because it flows. Glass wouldn't win any flowing contests, however. It makes treacle look like a speed demon, since it might take a hundred years to move a centimetre. But move it does, and in time you can see it in places like old windowpanes, which are much thicker at the bottom than the top.

Most of the fluids you are familiar with, such as air and water, share other properties as well. For one thing, they exert pressure in all directions including *upwards*, which surprises some people. Another fooler is the fact that fluid pressure is equal in all directions. Unexpected behaviour like this makes a perfect set-up for a con game. So we have included lots of 'pressure tactics' in this chapter.

Fluids also stick together. This clinging tendency, called 'cohesion', is strongest at the surface, where it acts like an invisible skin. And as soon as you've got invisible anything, you can fool people.

Fluids are adhesive, too. This ability to stick to other things is often totally unexpected. In this chapter, we'll show you how to make water act just like glue. You'll be stuck for the answer!

MAKE A SUCKER OF SUCKERS

The Set-up: Put two straws in your mouth. Stick the free end of one in a glass of lemonade. Keep the second straw outside the glass. Now try to drink the lemonade through the straw. (Note: It is considered cheating to put your tongue over the end of the straw that's outside the glass or to cover this straw with your finger.)

The Trick: You can suck till your cheeks meet but the lemonade will not reach your mouth. Ordinarily, when you drink through a straw, your mouth becomes a vacuum pump, lowering the air pressure in your mouth. Because air pressure tends to equalize, the now greater air pressure of the atmosphere pushes down on the surface of the drink, pushing it up the straw into your mouth.

47

In this stunt, the open straw keeps you from forming a vacuum pump with your mouth. Vacuum pumps won't work if they are not airtight. The straw is a leak in the system. Since the pressure in your mouth remains the same as the atmospheric pressure, the drink stays in the glass.

ANOTHER BET FOR SUCKERS

BET YOU CAN'T SUCK WATER FROM A JAR!

The Set-up: Ask an adult to make a hole large enough for a straw in the screw-top of a jar. Insert a straw and seal the connection with modelling clay or putty. Fill the jar to the brim with water. Screw on the cover with the straw in place. Now try to drink the water through the straw!

The Trick: In this stunt you *can* make a partial vacuum in your mouth. But you won't suck up the water because the surface of the water is not in contact with the atmosphere, so no air pressure can push the water into your mouth. A strong mechanical vacuum pump might be able to draw out the water, but the straw would probably collapse first. Your mouth can never create enough suction to win this sucker bet.

Take-away drink containers, with plastic lids with holes in the centre are not airtight. That's why you can still sip through the straw.

LOADED WORDS

BET YOU CAN'T FLIP A NEWSPAPER INTO THE AIR WITH A RULER!

The Set-up: Lay several sheets of full-sized newspaper (not the tabloid size) on a table. Choose a smooth-surfaced table, not one with a tablecloth. Position the

paper so that the long edge runs along the edge of the table. Put a wooden metre-rule or ruler under the newspaper so that half of it sticks out over the edge of the table. Smooth the papers flat. Now try to flip the newspaper half a metre into the air by striking the ruler with a single, quick blow.

The Trick: That newspaper is not going anywhere. Here's why. When you smooth the newspaper flat against the table, there is almost no air underneath it. All the pressure of the air is now on top of the paper and it's considerable. The total weight of air pressure on the surface of a single sheet of newspaper is about 10,000 pounds. The fast motion you need to flip the paper pits the ruler against the full 10,000 pounds of air, and the ruler breaks.

Of course, you can lift the paper by slowly hitting

the ruler. When you do this, air seeps under the paper, the pressure equalizes, and the paper can easily be lifted. However, a gentle tap on the ruler will never flip the paper.

THE LEAK-PROOF HOLE

BET YOU CAN'T MAKE WATER LEAK OUT OF A HOLE IN A BOTTLE!

The Set-up: Get a pair of scissors and a plastic bottle with a screw-top. Ask an adult to make a small hole in the side of the bottle near the bottom with the point of the scissors. Cover the hole with your finger while you fill the bottle with water to the brim. (Do this over the sink.) Screw on the top, making sure there is no air in the bottle. Take your finger away from the hole. Stand back and watch for the water to come pouring out!

The Trick: No water? That's because the odds were stacked against it. For water to leak out of the hole, the air pressure pushing on the water has to be less than the force of gravity. Usually the pressure on top of a liquid is equal to the air pressure pushing on the hole. The two forces cancel each other out; gravity wins and the water rushes forth. (Open the top of the bottle and see this happen.) But as long as the surface of the water is protected from air pressure by the bottle cap, air pressure works to keep the water *in* the bottle. Air pressure then wins because it is stronger than the force of gravity!

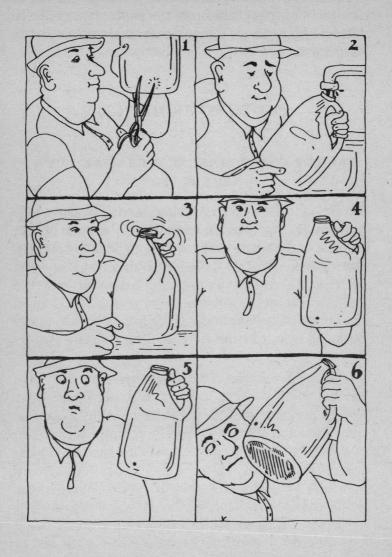

You have something else working against you here, too. It's the surface tension of the water. It acts like a skin and holds the water together. It's a weak force, but it works for you when you have a small hole.

BLOWING A CHANCE

BET YOU CAN'T BLOW UP A BALLOON IN A BOTTLE!

The Set-up: Select a balloon that is easy to blow up. Put it in an empty bottle and stretch the neck of the balloon completely over the mouth of the bottle. Try to blow up the balloon so it fills the bottle.

The Trick: So you thought this one would be easy? It's not only difficult, it's downright impossible. To inflate the balloon, you would need to compress the air trapped between the balloon and the bottle. To compress air requires force. Human lungs are not strong enough to inflate the balloon *and* to compress the trapped air.

A BREATHTAKING CHANCE

BET YOU CAN'T BLOW A WAD OF PAPER INTO A BOTTLE!

The Set-up: Place an empty bottle on its side. Put a small wad of paper in the neck. Try to blow the paper into the bottle.

The Trick: Not only won't the wad go in, it will fly out at you instead! When you blow into an enclosed space like a bottle, you increase the air pressure inside. Since

pressure will equalize when it can, the air rushes out of the bottle, taking the wad of paper with it. Amazing, but that's the way it flows!

THE ODDS AGAINST BLOWING UP

The Set-up: You will need two identical balloons that you have blown up a few times so you know they inflate easily, a 10-centimetre length of rubber or plastic tubing, a clothes-peg and two small rubber bands. Fold the tube in half and pinch the halves together with the clamp. This creates an airtight seal. Blow up one of the balloons so that it is almost fully inflated. Attach the neck to one end of the tubing with a rubber band. (This may take several tries before you get an airtight connection.) Inflate the second balloon slightly and attach it to the other end of the tubing with the remaining rubber band. Open the clothes-peg, allowing the air to pass freely from one balloon to the other.

The Trick: It isn't magic but a scientific law that keeps the two balloons from ending up the same size. The small balloon will always empty its contents into the large balloon.

Fluids in a flexible container assume a shape that has the smallest surface area. A single large sphere has less surface area than two smaller spheres whose contents equal the single large one. Since one large

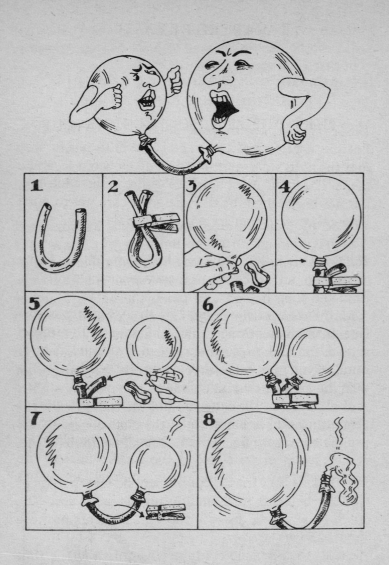

balloon has less surface area than two balloons containing the same amount of air, the small balloon empties its contents into the larger one.

WASTED BREATH

BET YOU CAN'T BLOW OUT A CANDLE THROUGH A FUNNEL!

The Set-up: Check with an adult before doing this trick. Put the narrow end of a metal funnel (a plastic one may burn) to your mouth and try to blow out a candle flame. The flame must be in the centre of the wide end, but not inside the funnel. Take great care not to burn yourself or anything else with the candle.

The Trick: No matter how you huff and puff, the flame doesn't go out. Instead it strangely flickers *towards* the funnel!

Many fluids have a tendency to flow along a surface. In this case, the air that is blown into the funnel spreads out and hugs the surface of the funnel. Almost none of your breath travels down the centre. This is why the flame is not extinguished.

The flame flickers *towards* the funnel because of another strange fluid phenomenon called the Bernoulli principle. According to this principle, moving air creates lower pressure along the surface next to the current. When you blow into the funnel, air rushes

along the sides and creates a low-pressure area in the centre. Any time a low-pressure area exists, air will rush in to equalize the pressure if it can. The flame is in the path of this rush of air, so it leans towards the mouth of the funnel. The next three tricks are also based on the Bernoulli effect.

BLOW-OUT PROOF

BET YOU CAN'T BLOW A PING-PONG BALL OUT OF A FUNNEL!

The Set-up: Put a Ping-Pong ball in a funnel. Tilt your head back and try to blow the ball out of the funnel. Blow with a steady pressure, not with short bursts.

The Trick: The most frustrating part of this bet is that the harder you try to blow the ball out, the more firmly it stays in place! This stunt is a classic example of the Bernoulli effect. Moving air exerts decreased pressure at right angles to the direction of motion. In this

case, the rushing air coming out of the funnel hits the surface of the ball. Air rushes around the ball, creating lower pressure on the underside of the ball. The greater pressure of the atmosphere becomes immediately apparent. It holds the ball in the funnel. So the harder you blow, the more you reduce the pressure under the ball and the more firmly the ball is pushed by atmospheric pressure into the funnel.

NO WINDFALL HERE

BET YOU CAN'T BLOW A PIECE OF PAPER OFF THE END OF A REEL!

The Set-up: You will need a 5-centimetre square of paper, a pin, some Sellotape, and a reel of thread. Put the pin through the centre of the paper and tape it in place. Insert the pin in the centre of the reel of thread. Tilt the reel upwards slightly as you put the open end to your lips. Try to blow the paper off the end of the reel! Blow with a steady pressure not with short bursts.

Be careful the pin doesn't protrude all the way through the reel into your mouth!

The Trick: The Bernoulli effect makes this an impossible task. The harder you blow, the more securely the paper is drawn against the top of the reel. Air rushes out of the hole, spreads between the paper and the reel and, as in the last two tricks, reduces the air pressure. The greater atmospheric pressure on the other side of the paper presses down and holds it firmly against the top of the reel. You lose.

UP AGAINST THE ODDS

BET YOU CAN'T BLOW A STRIP OF PAPER DOWN TOWARDS YOUR TOES!

The Trick: Cut a strip of ordinary paper about 28 centimetres long and 5 centimetres wide. Hold one end

just below your lower lip. Blow down on the paper. Try to make it point towards your toes.

The Trick: The paper is going to rise towards your nose, not droop towards your toes! This apparently simple gimmick is the key to flight. It demonstrates the lifting properties of the Bernoulli effect. Air rushing across the top of the paper reduces the pressure. The air under the paper, at the greater pressure of the atmosphere, pushes upwards and lifts the paper.

Engineers use this principle in the design of aeroplane wings. A wing is shaped so that air rushes over the top of the wing faster than it passes under the bottom. The greater pressure on the underside of the wing lifts the plane into the air.

SUM IS LESS THAN MORE

BET YOU CAN'T MIX ONE LITRE WITH ONE LITRE AND GET TWO LITRES!

The Set-up: You will need a large measuring jug, a 3-litre pot or bowl, a spoon, a litre of surgical spirit and a litre of water. Put a litre of water in the pot. (Measure carefully!) Pour in one litre of surgical spirit. (Again, measure carefully!) Stir the mixture well. Now measure the volume of the mixture with the measuring jug. Did you get two litres?

The Trick: If you didn't get two litres, it's not because you are a sloppy measurer. The two liquids combine to measure noticeably less than two litres! Why?

The disappearing liquid is due to the space between the molecules of water and the surgical spirit, or alcohol. When these two particular liquids are mixed, the alcohol molecules slip between the spaces of the water molecules, making a smaller combined volume for the two liquids. Not all combinations of liquids will give this strange shrinking illusion, but water and alcohol are good foolers.

WATERTIGHT

BET YOU CAN'T PULL APART TWO WET GLASSES!

The Set-up: You will need two heavy plastic water glasses that are the same size. Put one inside the other. Drip water around the rim of the outer glass so that a thin layer of water forms between the two glasses. Try to separate them by pulling them apart.

The Trick: The water acts like glue, holding the glasses together. Nature has put in a double fix here. The first is 'cohesion', which is the force pulling water molecules together. The second is 'adhesion', which is the attraction between water and the glass. Only in a tiny place like the one between the glasses can they combine to form such a powerful bond.

Since you have those two glasses stuck together, it's only fair play to tell you the secret of how to get them apart. Cool the inner glass by filling it with ice-water. While the ice-water is still in the inner glass, run hot water around the outside glass and *immediately* pull them apart. If you don't act quickly, the glasses will stick even more tightly. The outer glass expands from the heat and the inner one contracts from the ice-water. The small difference in size is large enough to break the seal of the water so you can pull the glasses apart.

FLOATING ODDS

BET YOU CAN'T MAKE A CORK FLOAT IN THE CENTRE OF A GLASS OF WATER!

The Set-up: Fill a glass with water. Now overfill it by adding water slowly until the surface rises over the edge of the glass. Gently set a cork afloat in the centre. Try to keep it there!

The Trick: That cork is going to move towards an edge no matter how many times you push it back towards the middle. Water molecules cling together. One evidence of this cohesive force is called surface tension. It's like an invisible skin. The cork must break the surface tension of the water and it does this where the force is weakest, usually the lowest point of the liquid. In this case, the lowest point of the water is the edge. If you view the glass at eye-level, you can see that the water has a bulging shape that rises in the centre.

Now as long as you're playing around with that cork, try this one.

BET YOU CAN'T MAKE A CORK FLOAT NEAR THE EDGE OF A GLASS OF WATER!

The Set-up: Empty some of the water from the overfull glass so that the surface of the water is well below the rim of the glass. Gently put the cork in the water. Guide it to an edge if you like. Try to get the cork to float near the edge.

The Trick: The cork is always going to end up in the centre. Two forces work against you here. One is surface tension again. The other is a force of attraction between the water and the glass. The water sticks to the glass and wets it, pulling the surface up at the edges. The cork breaks the surface tension where it is weakest, and, in this case, it is the centre, the point where the water level is lowest.

COMING UP EMPTY

BET YOU CAN'T POUR WATER THROUGH A HOSE!

The Set-up: You will need a garden hose that is at least 1.5 centimetres in diameter, a reel for storing the hose that is at least 30 centimetres in diameter, a funnel, a bucket of water, and an empty bucket. Coil the hose at least five times around the reel. The hose should be completely empty and have no kinks. Put one end of the hose in the empty bucket. Hold the other end several feet above the reel. Insert the funnel in this end

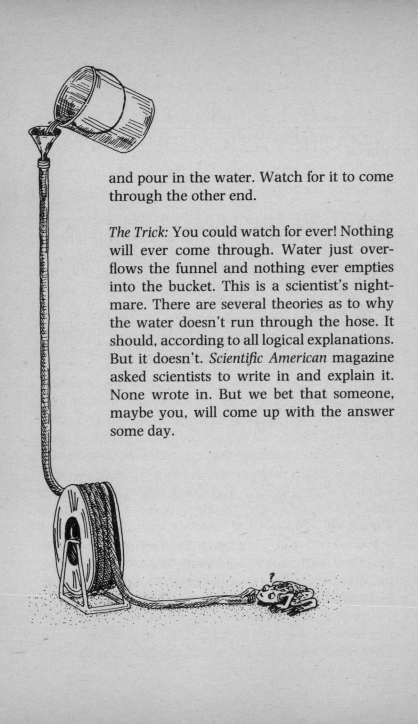

and pour in the water. Watch for it to come through the other end.

The Trick: You could watch for ever! Nothing will ever come through. Water just overflows the funnel and nothing ever empties into the bucket. This is a scientist's nightmare. There are several theories as to why the water doesn't run through the hose. It should, according to all logical explanations. But it doesn't. *Scientific American* magazine asked scientists to write in and explain it. None wrote in. But we bet that someone, maybe you, will come up with the answer some day.

4

MATHEMATICAL DUPLICITY

DON'T SKIP THIS CHAPTER! We know most people hate numbers and think arithmetic is boring, so we didn't put any addition, subtraction, multiplication or division games here. What's left? Lots. Arithmetic is only part of mathematics. Betting on tricks is maths. The calculation of odds is called probability and it belongs to a branch of mathematics called statistics. Even fixed bets, like the ones in this book, can be expressed mathematically. They are 'beyond chance'.

Some branches of mathematics don't use numbers at all. Take topology, the mathematics of form and shape. It's fascinating. We are going to fool you with topological oddities, like a strip of paper that has only one side and a banknote that mysteriously transfers its curves to other objects. Actually, you are probably familiar with topology and don't know it. If you've done mazes or solved jigsaw puzzles, you are into topological games.

We're betting you are into a lot of other kinds of no-numbers mathematics and don't know it. What you still don't know about sequence and progressions can fool you. Let us count the ways!

CLIP-JOINT

BET YOU CAN'T KEEP TWO PAPER CLIPS FROM HOOKING TOGETHER!

The Set-up: You will need a banknote and two paper clips for this trick. Fold a banknote into a flattened 'S' shape. Hold it so that you are looking down on the 'S'. Take a paper clip and hook the short, single wire over two thicknesses of the note. Hook the short, single wire of a second paper clip over two thicknesses of paper on the other side of the curve of the note as shown in the picture. Now straighten the note by grasping the ends and pulling sharply. The two paper clips will fly into the air and hook together.

The Trick: Although the two paper clips are not touching on the note, they miraculously hook together when you snap it. This stunt is based on a topological phenomenon called transference of curves. The 'S'-shaped curve made by the folds in the banknote is transferred to the paper clips when the note is straightened.

If the exact mechanism of this oddity interests you, pull slowly on the ends of the note. You may be able to see what is happening. The trick doesn't always work when the note is pulled slowly, but sometimes it does. So don't make any bets on the slow move.

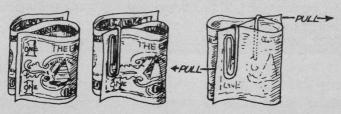

OUT OF ORDER

BET YOU CAN'T FLIP AND TURN A BOOK AND MAKE IT END UP IN THE SAME POSITION AS WHEN YOU TURN AND FLIP IT!

The Set-up: Hold a book in your hands as if you are going to read the front cover. Flip it over from bottom to top. Then turn it 90° in a counter-clockwise direction. You will end up with the spine facing you and the back cover on top.

Now hold the book as if you are going to read it again. The same two operations are going to be performed, but in reverse order. Turn the book 90° in a counter-clockwise direction. Flip it over, bottom to top. The back cover will be on top, but the spine now faces away from you.

The Trick: Sequence is the key word in understanding why this trick doesn't work. In a sequence involving two different kinds of operations (and flips and turns are two different kinds of operations), the sequence of the operations will affect the outcome. Wonder why we put this in the maths chapter? It belongs here, all right, for direction of motion and position are mathematical properties.

CURSES, COILED AGAIN

There is an old carnival trick that has fooled people for hundreds of years. It's based on topology, a part of mathematics. You can still find candidates for this bet. It involves nothing more difficult than trapping a belt around a pencil.

The Set-up: You will need a belt that has distinctly different surfaces on the inside and the outside. Fold the belt in half with the inside surfaces together. Coil the belt, beginning with the folded end, to form a flat circle. The centre of the coil has an 'S' shape. One loop of this 'S' is formed by the belt's inside and the other by the belt's outside. Put a pencil in the half of the 'S' curve formed by the inside surfaces. Grasp both ends of the belt and pull. The belt will unwind, but it will be held by the pencil. You are now ready to do the old garter con. Say:

BET YOU CAN'T CATCH THE BELT WITH THE PENCIL LIKE I SHOWED YOU!

The Set-up: In spite of what you've demonstrated, no matter where your friend places the pencil, you can pull the belt free. Here's how the trick is rigged:

1. If the pencil is placed in the half of the 'S' that is the outside of the belt, just hold the ends and pull the belt free.
2. If the pencil is placed on the inside curve, take one end of the belt and unwind it a turn. Now grasp both ends and pull. The belt slips free. (You'll give

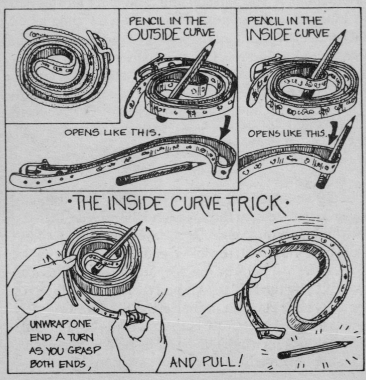

PENCIL IN THE OUTSIDE CURVE

PENCIL IN THE INSIDE CURVE

OPENS LIKE THIS.

OPENS LIKE THIS.

·THE INSIDE CURVE TRICK·

UNWRAP ONE END A TURN AS YOU GRASP BOTH ENDS,

AND PULL!

away the secret of this trick if you make the unwinding too obvious. Pretend you are straightening up the coils.) By unwrapping one end, you are folding the belt the other way. The inside is now the outside. The manipulation is so far away from the original fold that it isn't obvious what you have done.

NO LOOPHOLE HERE

BET YOU CAN'T CUT A PAPER LOOP INTO TWO PIECES!

The Set-up: You will need some newspaper, scissors, and tape or glue. Cut a strip of newspaper about 5 centimetres wide. Turn over one end of the strip, then tape the two ends together to form a loop. Now try to divide the loop into two pieces by cutting lengthwise down the centre of the strip. Be careful with the scissors.

TURN ONE END ONCE AND TAPE.

CUT HERE

The Trick: When you have finished cutting you will still have a single loop, but it will be twice as long as the original. That's because the twisted loop is a topological oddity called a Möbius strip. It has only one side. Really! No top and no bottom, just one side. Make another Möbius strip and draw a pencil line down the centre. You will cover all the surface of the paper and end up at the beginning point.

Don't go away. We offer you another challenge.

BET YOU CAN'T MAKE THE SAME FIGURE IF YOU CUT THE LOOP IN A DIFFERENT SPOT!

The Set-up: This time you are to cut the strip about one third of the distance from the edge, instead of at the half-way point. Cut the entire strip, keeping the same distance from the edge.

CUT HERE

Please, just one more Möbius trick!

The Trick: You don't win this time because the Möbius strip has more than one surprise. When cut at one third of the width, the resulting figure is a loop twice as long as the original, but, incredibly, there is a loop the same size as the original linked to the longer one.

BET YOU CAN'T CUT DOWN THE CENTRE OF A MÖBIUS STRIP AND GET A LOOP TWICE AS LONG AS THE ORIGINAL!

The Set-up: This may seem to be the same bet as the first one, but we are going to make a double Möbius strip this time. Cut another 5-centimetre-wide newspaper strip and turn one end so that it makes a complete revolution (two twists) before you tape it. Now cut the double Möbius down the centre.

The Trick: Again the Möbius amazes. This time you get

TURN ONE END TWICE, AND TAPE.

CUT HERE.

two loops the same length as the original but linked together. If you now cut those loops down the centre, you will end up with four loops all the same size as the original and all linked together.

Warning: Playing with Möbius strips may be habit-forming, but it is not injurious to your health.

ON PAPER THE ODDS LOOK GOOD ... BUT

BET YOU CAN'T FOLD A PIECE OF PAPER IN HALF MORE THAN NINE TIMES!

The Set-up: This challenge has no restrictions. All you have to do is fold a piece of paper in half more than nine times. Use any kind of paper, any size, and any thickness – as long as it can be folded in half. Divide the paper in half evenly on each fold. The folds may be

in any direction: lengthwise, crosswise, or even on a diagonal. Try it. We dare you. This is such a sure thing, we even double dare you.

The Trick: The way the number of pieces of paper included in a fold increases is called a geometrical progression. On the first fold you have two pieces of paper, on the second, four. The third fold creates eight layers. By the time you make the seventh fold you are trying to crease 128 separate sheets. It's like trying to fold a book! More than nine folds and it's impossible.

BOTTOMS UP

BET YOU CAN'T GET THREE CUPS FACING UP!

The Set-up: This is an old carnival game with a real con in it. Place three cups in a row. The two end cups should face down and the centre cup should face up. Now make them all face up in three moves, each move reversing two cups. Remember, three moves, no more and no less.

Solution: 1. A and B
2. A and C
3. A and B

Now here's the con. Keep the two end cups facing upwards, but turn the centre cup upside-down. Say:

77

(THE CORRECT SET-UP)

(THE CON)

78

BET YOU CAN'T GET THE THREE CUPS FACING UP!

The Trick: The reason you can do this trick and no one else can is because you have changed the situation. Although there are still two cups in one direction and one in the opposite direction, the positions are reversed. In three moves you can get all three cups upside-down, but you can't get all three facing up. Don't try this more than once on an audience, for someone is sure to catch the switch.

THE WILL THAT WOULDN'T

BET YOU CAN'T DIVIDE BY FIVE!

The Set-up: This challenge is really a map puzzle. To win, you must draw a map that solves this story puzzle.

A farmer had five sons. When he died, his will had these instructions for the division of his land among the sons:

1. Each son had to be a neighbour to all the others.
2. The land of any two brothers had to have at least one edge in common, not just a point.
3. Each brother's land had to be in one piece.

The Trick: It seems that five figures, no matter what their size or shape, cannot share common sides. Ferdinand Möbius the topologist who devised the Möbius strip, thought up this puzzle more than a hundred years ago. If there is an answer to it, no mathematician

has discovered it, including the genius who dreamed it up.

This topographical oddity has been put to practical use, though. Mapmakers can show any number of separate regions with only four colours because of the fact that only four regions can share a common side.

PICKING UP LOOSE CHANGE

BET YOU CAN'T PICK UP THE LAST COIN IN THIS GAME!

The Set-up: This fooler is a two-person game played

with twenty coins. Each player takes turns picking up one, two or three coins. The one who picks up the last coin is the winner.

The Trick: The con is set into action by insisting that your opponent goes first. Now, if you can count to four, you are the winner. The trick is based on a simple mathematical calculation – multiples of four. The number of coins you take each time depends upon how many coins your opponent takes. The total for the combined moves must be four. (If your opponent takes three coins, you take one. If two are removed, you take two.) By going second you keep the number of remaining coins divisible by four. On your opponent's fifth turn, there will be four coins remaining. Since three is the maximum number that can be picked up on a single move, you win!

TIME'S UP

We promised no number games, but this is an exception to the rule that arithmetic is dull. It's too good to pass up because it's wonderfully simple and a perfect sure-win bet. Try it!

The Set-up: Here is the problem to be solved.

You are to travel from Point A to Point B and return. On the trip from A to B, you travel at 30 kilometres per hour. How fast would you have to travel from B to A in order to average 60 kilometres per hour for the round trip?

The Trick: The answer everyone quickly gives is 90 kilometres an hour. Wrong! This is an impossible journey. Think of it this way: imagine that the distance from A to B is 1 kilometre. Sixty kilometres per hour is 1 kilometre a minute. So it would take two minutes at the average speed of 60 kilometres per hour to make the round trip of 2 kilometres. Now, the first half of the trip – 1 kilometre – is to be made at 30 kilometres per hour. This would take two minutes. You can see there is no time left for the return trip.

5

ENERGY ENTRAPMENTS

In nature, there's no such thing as an energy crisis. Conservation of energy is rigorously observed. Energy input always equals energy output. It's a natural law. The world may run out of fuel, but it won't run out of energy. Does this surprise you? There's a loophole in the law that can trick you: nature doesn't care what form energy takes.

Heat, light, sound, electricity and motion are all forms of energy. One can be changed into another. Rub your hands together and feel motion transformed into heat. Sometimes, however, it's not easy to detect an energy transformation. It may look like energy is disappearing. And appearances can deceive you.

Energy is defined in science as the ability to do work. Physicists measure it in terms of mass moved through a distance. Energy can be found in all chemical reactions. Some take in energy and store it; others release energy. Energy foolers include pressure, which can do the same kinds of jobs as heat, and light that's out of sight.

For your entertainment, we are going to take energy and bend it, twist it, bounce it, burn it, and even extinguish it. Here's *our* law: energy generates fun!

NOT A BURNING QUESTION

BET YOU CAN'T KEEP A MATCH BURNING
OVER A GLASS OF LEMONADE!

The Set-up: Check with an adult in your house before doing this trick, which involves fire. You will need a fresh bottle of lemonade and a match. Pour the lemonade into a glass. Light a wooden match and hold it over the glass. Be careful not to burn your fingers!

The Trick: The warning about burning your fingers is our little joke. There is no chance your fingers will get burned. The match is quickly extinguished when you hold it close to the lemonade. This is because the lemonade contains carbon dioxide gas under pressure. When the bottle is opened, the bubbles of gas burst at the surface and the area just above the glass becomes rich in carbon dioxide and poor in oxygen. Fire is heat and light energy that is released when a fuel is combined with oxygen. Remove the oxygen and the reaction stops. In this case, the match quickly burns up whatever oxygen there is in the vicinity and only carbon dioxide, which won't support combustion, remains. So the match goes out.

Note: This trick requires a bottle of freshly opened lemonade. The wager will fall flat if the beverage is flat!

FOLLOW THE BOUNCING BALL-POINT

BET YOU CAN'T GET A SUPERBALL TO BOUNCE AS HIGH AS A PEN!

They will both be dropped on to the same surface, from the same height, and with the same force.

The Set-up: You will need a Superball and a ball-point pen. Stab the point of the pen into the Superball. Insert it deeply enough so that the ball won't drop off when you hold only the pen, but don't jam the entire tip into the ball.

Hold the end of the pen at arm's length. The ball should be facing down. (YOU MUST TAKE TWO SAFETY PRECAUTIONS AT THIS POINT: FIRST, CHECK TO MAKE SURE YOU ARE NOT STANDING BENEATH A CEILING LIGHT FIXTURE, AND SECONDLY, COVER YOUR EYES WITH YOUR HAND AND PEEK OUT THROUGH A TINY CRACK.) Now you are ready. Drop the pen. WATCH OUT! Which bounced higher – the ball or the pen?

The Trick: The pen rockets out of the ball. If you are indoors, it will hit the ceiling. The Superball either doesn't bounce at all or just a fraction of what it normally does. Usually the Superball bounces to 90 per cent of the height it was dropped from, losing very little of its kinetic energy, or motion energy. But when it is dropped in tandem with the pen, the collision affects both the ball and the pen. If there were no pen, the kinetic energy of the impact would show up in the bounce of the ball. In this case, some of the kinetic energy of the ball is transferred to the pen, which really takes off. This happens because the pen has a smaller mass (weight) than the ball. Thus, it can travel nine times as high as the ball from the same amount of kinetic energy.

NO STRAINING ALLOWED

BET YOU CAN'T MAKE A FLAME PASS THROUGH A SIEVE!

The Set-up: Check with an adult in your house before doing this trick, which involves fire. You will need a candle and a sieve. (Do not use a plastic sieve because it could catch fire.) Light the candle. Hold the sieve over the flame. Try to make the flame pass through the wire grid. There are plenty of holes, so this should be easy. Right?

The Trick: It's not easy. In fact, it's impossible. The sieve may be full of holes, but the flame stops beneath it. A visible flame is a combination of both heat and light energy given off by the burning gases. But the metal sieve absorbs the heat energy. Without heat energy, the gases cannot maintain kindling point (the temperature necessary to initiate combustion) and all the combustion is done below the source of heat diversion (the sieve). View the effect from the side. You will see that the light of the flame stops at the sieve, but smoke from the burning gases passes freely through the holes.

NOTHING TO GET BURNT UP ABOUT

BET YOU CAN'T BURN A HOLE IN THE BOTTOM OF A PAPER CUP!

The Set-up: Check with an adult in your house before doing this trick, which involves fire. If you get the go-ahead, do the stunt over the sink, for safety's sake. Fill a paper cup with water. Light a wooden match and hold it under the centre of the paper cup. Try to burn a hole in the paper cup.

The Trick: Paper cups really do burn. The tricker here is the water. It takes four things to start a fire: fuel, a supply of oxygen, a source of heat, and a kindling point (the temperature at which a fuel will ignite). It's

obvious you have fuel (the paper cup). There's plenty of oxygen (about one fifth of the air). And you have a heat source (the match). What's missing is the kindling point. The water in the cup draws the heat energy away from the paper and it never reaches the temperature necessary for ignition.

A COLD FACT

BET YOU CAN'T CUT AN ICE BLOCK IN TWO WITH A WIRE!

The Set-up: Remove the separator from an ice-cube tray and fill the tray with water. Freeze it overnight. Remove the block of ice from the tray and suspend it between two tins. Do this in the sink or a flat dish, because there will be dripping water. Tie a loop of very thin wire around the ice. Hang a brick or other heavy weight to the wire. The wire will slowly cut through the ice. When it cuts through, do you have two pieces?

The Trick: Surprisingly, the wire cuts completely through the ice block, but it still remains in one piece. The wire cuts the ice because of pressure, a force over an area, that is transformed into heat energy. As the wire presses against the ice, the part directly below the wire melts. The melted ice directly above the wire refreezes, even when the air temperature is well above the freezing point.

The water is able to refreeze because the inside of the ice block is several degrees below the freezing point.

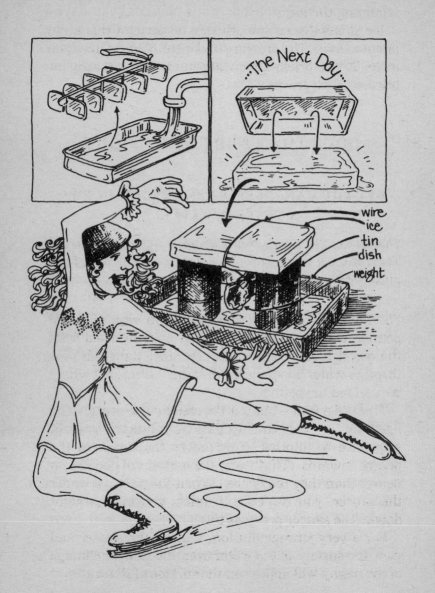

...The Next Day...

wire
ice
tin
dish
weight

The heat of the wire is transferred to this cold area, refreezing the ice.

Ice skaters get a smooth ride because of this same phenomenon. The pressure under the blade of the skate melts the ice briefly. The water under their skates 'lubricates' their tracks.

ODDS THAT ARE OUT OF SIGHT

BET YOU CAN'T SEE A PENNY THROUGH A GLASS OF WATER!

The Set-up: Fill a glass with water – right to the brim. Then place it on top of a 1p coin. Cover the top of the glass with a saucer. Can you see the penny?

The Trick: Don't strain your eyes! You won't see the penny. In order to see something, light reflected from the object must reach your eyes. Since light can pass through water, it's puzzling that there is no spot where we can see the penny.

There is a spot – but it is covered by the saucer. The light rays are bent as they pass from one transparent substance to another. This moves the image of the penny upwards. (That's why the bottoms of pools seem nearer than they really are.) When the penny is under the saucer, you can't see it unless you look straight down. The saucer prevents this.

For a very strange illusion, remove the saucer and view the surface of the water from the side. The image of the penny will appear on the surface of the water.

BE SURE THE BASE OF THE GLASS ISN'T A THICK ONE. OTHERWISE THE PENNY WILL BE VISIBLE.

COOL UNDER FIRE

The Set-up: For this wager, ice-water is defined as water with ice in it. To begin, you will need a tray of ice-cubes, a saucepan, a weather thermometer, a spoon, and some water. Put the ice-cubes in the saucepan with 13 to 15 centimetres of water. Stir the mixture with the thermometer. It should read 32 °F or 0 °C. Make sure that the bulb of the thermometer is completely submerged and that it is not touching the sides or bottom of the pan.

Place the pan over a low heat for a minute. (Check with an adult before using the cooker.) Turn off the cooker and stir the ice-water thoroughly. Again take a temperature reading, making sure the bulb is suspended in the liquid and not touching the pan. If the temperature has not been raised, heat the mixture again until the ice is almost melted. Stir and take another temperature reading. Has the temperature been raised? When the ice is melted, you are finished. The mixture is no longer ice-water.

The Trick: As long as there is ice in the water, the temperature will stay 32 °F or 0 °C. The heat you put into the pot did not just disappear. All of the energy was used to melt the ice. Not a single bit went to warm the water. When the ice is gone, of course, the heat will produce a change in the temperature of the water.

6

MIND AND BODY CON GAMES

Don't believe what you see or trust what you hear, smell or feel as you do the tricks in this chapter. Your senses can fool you. So can your body. The way you perceive the world is not always the way it really is.

Each of these specialized con games is a trip into the world of inner space – your own mind and body. You'll think you have taken leave of your senses as we trick your eyes with an optical illusion, prove that the hand is not always quicker than the eye, fix it so one hand doesn't know what the other is doing, and set it up so that your body will disobey your mind.

Part of the way you act and react is governed by unconscious senses, like proprioception. By pitting your conscious senses against the unconscious ones, we'll confuse you even further.

The workings of the brain are mysterious, but so are the body's physical capabilities. You probably don't know a lot of things about yourself. Sneakily, we have used our knowledge of your body's limitations against you.

Humans aren't foolproof, but these tricks are. Only you can do them . . . and you're on your own!

BIG MONEY

BET YOU CAN'T FIT A PENNY ON THIS DRAWING OF A TABLE!

The Set-up: Try to fit a 1p coin on this picture of a table so that it doesn't touch any of the edges.

The Trick: It doesn't fit, does it? Here's what fools you. The table is a parallelogram, not a rectangle as we see it. We think the penny will fit because a rectangle with sides the same length as the parallelogram would be large enough for the penny to fit inside comfortably.

OUT OF TOUCH WITH REALITY

BET YOU CAN'T TELL HOT FROM COLD!

The Set-up: You will need three bowls of water: one cold, one very warm, and one at room temperature. Soak your left hand in the cold water and your right hand in the hot water for about three minutes. Then, plunge both hands into the bowl of room temperature water. Is the water hot or cold?

The Trick: You will not be able to answer because the water feels both hot *and* cold. The brain is getting conflicting signals from your hands. One says the water is cold; the other says it's hot. You will be thoroughly confused.

Hot and cold are relative terms and they depend on what you use as a reference. Here you use two different references. The hand that has been in the cold water now feels hot. The hand that's been in the hot water now feels cold.

MISSING THE POINT

BET YOU CAN'T MAKE TWO PENCIL POINTS
MEET IN ONE TRY!

The Set-up: Take a sharp pencil in each hand. Hold

your hands about 60 centimetres apart and with the pencil points facing each other. Close one eye. Keep it closed! Now try to get the points to meet.

The Trick: This trick proves that you can't always believe your eyes. You can't bring the points together because you lack binocular vision (vision from two separate vantage points), which allows you to calculate the distance of an object. When one eye is covered, the familiar depth cues are missing. Depth perception is most difficult on objects as close together as the pencils. And the margin for error with targets as small as the pencil points is enormous.

Practice will make you perfect in this stunt. The body learns other ways to judge depth when given practice. See if you can get the pencil points to meet after a few more tries. Bet you can!

TIGHT WAD'S DILEMMA

BET YOU CAN'T CRUMPLE A SHEET OF NEWS-
PAPER INTO A WAD WITH ONE HAND!

The Set-up: Take a double-page sheet of newspaper and
crumple it into a tightly compressed ball. Use both
hands. Set this ball aside. With one hand, grasp the
edge of another double-page sheet of newspaper and
try to crumple it into the same tightly packed ball.
This time you must use only one hand for the task.
The newspaper may not be pushed against anything
and you must get the same-sized ball you got with the
two-hand crush.

The Trick: Most people underestimate the size of a sheet of newspaper. It soon fills the normal-sized hand, leaving only the tips of a few fingers free to deliver power to crumple the remainder. Even if you are big-handed enough to wrinkle up the entire sheet, you will not be able to compress it. The fully extended hand cannot cover enough of the surface of the sphere-shaped wad. To compress a sphere, pressure must be exerted over most of the surface.

Note: Choose a subject with fairly small hands for this trick. A man with gigantic hands might come close enough to claim he is a winner.

TIME TO GET CRACKING

BET YOU CAN'T CRACK A KNUCKLE TWICE IN FIVE MINUTES!

The Set-up: Cracking your knuckles is easy, but we bet you can't crack any particular joint twice in five minutes. So take out your watch and get cracking. First, crack the joint until no more popping noises are heard. Then begin the timing. Another pop in the same knuckle within the five-minute limit wins.

The Trick: The minor medical mystery of knuckle cracking was solved in about 1970 by three British doctors. They discovered that the noise was caused by exploding gas bubbles. Joints have fluid in them containing dissolved gases. When the joint is stretched, the pressure is reduced and the gas bubbles pop out of the solution. (You've seen this phenomenon when a bottle of lemonade is opened.) The gas in knuckles can't escape from the joint. In about fifteen minutes, it is reabsorbed by the joint fluid. So you must wait a quarter of an hour before you can crack again!

EVEN-HANDEDNESS

BET YOU CAN'T MAKE YOUR FINGERS MEET UNDER A METRE-RULE AT ANY PLACE BUT THE CENTRE!

The Set-up: Rest the ends of a metre-rule on your index fingers. Slowly bring your fingers towards each other. They will meet at the exact centre (the 50-centimetre mark) every time. Try to make them meet at some other place.

The Trick: You prevent yourself from winning this trick. First of all, there is only one place under the metre-rule where it will balance on a single support: the centre of gravity. If your fingers meet anywhere else, the metre-rule will be off balance and fall. Consciously, you are trying to make your hands meet at some other point. But these efforts are overridden by an unconscious sense called proprioception. This complicated feedback system co-ordinates your body movements to maintain the balance of the ruler. The hundreds of amazing adjustments in hand position always result in the same thing – a balanced ruler supported at its centre of gravity.

TIGHT-FISTED ABOUT MONEY

BET YOU CAN'T DROP A PENNY HELD BETWEEN TWO FINGERS!

The Set-up: Place the tips of your ring-fingers together. Fold the other fingers down so the knuckles touch. Ask an assistant to put a 1p coin between the tips of your ring-fingers. Now try to open your fingers and drop the penny. You may not *slide* your fingers apart.

The Trick: The ring-fingers cannot move independently of the other fingers. Ligaments connect them to the other digits, especially the middle finger. When the middle finger is immobilized, so is the ring-finger. The penny is trapped.

Some people, especially pianists, have stretched the ligaments that control the free motion of the ring-fingers. When just the middle fingers are restricted, the ring-fingers can still move. However, if the knuckles of all three other fingers are made to touch, even musicians can't make the penny drop.

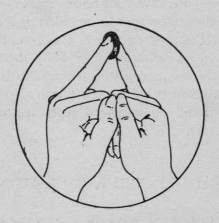

SHAKY ODDS

BET YOU CAN'T HOLD YOUR HAND STILL!

The Set-up: Unfold a paper clip. Smooth out all the bumps and bend it into a 'V' shape. Put the V upside-down on the back edge of a table knife. Hold the knife over a table with the ends of the wire resting lightly on the table. Try to hold the wire still.

Note: You may not rest your hand on the table or any other object.

The Trick: The strangest part about this 'walking wire' is that the harder you try to hold your hand still, the faster the wire walks down the back of the knife. Muscles are made up of cells that exist in alternating states of contraction and relaxation. When you contract your muscles to hold a position, only some muscle cells are in a state of contraction. Others are relaxing and recovering, getting ready to take their turn. This constant change-over creates a very slight motion or tremor that can't be seen easily. The walking wire magnifies this motion. The harder you try to hold your hand steady, the harder your muscles are working

and the greater the difference between the tensed and relaxed parts of the muscle.

QUICK BUCK

BET YOU CAN'T CATCH A BANKNOTE!

The Set-up: Put a lengthwise crease in a new banknote. Hold it at one end with your thumb and index finger. Have someone place their thumb and index finger around the note. They must now try to catch the note when you drop it.

The Trick: Here is one case where the hand is not quicker than the eye. Don't worry. Nobody is going to get their hands on your money, because their reflexes will be too slow. The catching mechanism works like this: the sight of the note dropping must register in the brain, which then sends a message to the fingers. Although this relay takes less than a second, it's too long.

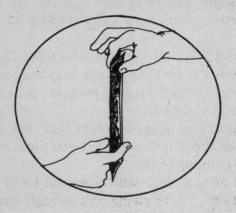

It is possible to catch a note on the drop, but only if you are the one dropping it. Your proprioceptive sense (sense of your own body movements) co-ordinates the movement of your hands. The hand that catches a ball reacts to the message activating the release, not the sight of the dropping ball. Sight is not involved when you are both dropper and catcher. Prove it by doing the drop/catch with your eyes closed.

7

PROBABLE PITFALLS AND CUNNING BLUFFS

The odds are against you in this chapter of 'almost impossible' tricks. But, unlike the other challenges, there is a slight chance of winning. We are offering you a sporting chance . . . even though it's a slim one.

These quick tricks are impossible for most. However, what is impossible for the majority *may* be possible for you. Consider yourself lucky if you can do even one. You have beaten the odds.

We are going to hedge our bets here, too. We bet that it will be *almost* impossible to resist these probable pitfalls and cunning bluffs.

You will need a clock with a second hand for the next two stunts. We're giving you enough time to be fooled . . . and *maybe* enough time to win.

1. Bet you can't write this number down! Get a pencil and paper. You have ten seconds. Ready? Write this number . . . eleven thousand, eleven hundred, and eleven.

   The answer is on p. 116.

2. You have ten seconds to study this picture. On your mark . . . go. Now stop looking. Bet you can't guess the number of dots in the circle!

The answer is on p. 116.

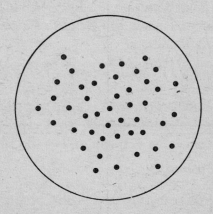

The first two 'gottcha's' were easy. If you think you're ready for the big time, try these.

3. Bet you can't guess how many times you would have to wrap a string around your head like a hat to equal your height!

The answer is on p. 116.

4. Bet you can't tell me which weighs more: a litre of wet sand or a litre of dry sand! No guessing allowed here. Be prepared to explain your answer.

The correct explanation is on p. 116.

Next are two stumpers to show how dense you are.

5. Bet you can't tell me which weighs more: a litre of milk or a litre of cream! Explain yourself.

   The correct explanation is on p. 116.

6. A cork floats in water. It's light, full of air. Right? Bet you can't guess the weight of a cork ball 1.5 metres in diameter!

   Look on p. 117 for the answer.

7. Here's a difficult test in decoding. The following set of letters is not random. They represent a logical sequence. Bet you can't fill in the blanks!

   O, T, T, F, F, S, –, –, –, –.

   The solution to this tantalizing problem is on p. 117.

Enough brain-teasers. Here are some bluffs to stretch your muscles.

8. Your brain is supposed to be connected to your mouth. Here's a tongue-twister that experts say is the world's most difficult. Perhaps a trained tongue can do it, but: bet you can't say 'Unique New York' three times quickly!

9. Bet you can't kiss your elbow! We hope you don't care if you look foolish. Try it. You may gain the respect of a contortionist.

10. You may need some pepper to test this one out. By the way, this really is impossible, not just im-

probable. Bet you can't sneeze with your eyes open!

11. Bet you can't hold something in your right hand that you can hold in your left! (It's not very heavy, either.) Give up? It's your right elbow, of course.

12. Get a nice juicy lemon. Suck on it. Are you all puckered up? Now ... bet you can't whistle a tune! A variation of this nearly impossible trick is to try to whistle while eating a cracker. But don't laugh while you try this or you'll be cleaning up cracker crumbs.

13. If you play this one straight, it's impossible. Carnival people put a twist on it and conned people. Make a pendulum half a metre long with a bob made from a ball. (You can ask an adult to attach it to the string with a nail through a knot or with a staple gun.) Set up a lemonade bottle as a target. Bet you can't swing the pendulum so that it hits the bottle on the return trip!

The explanation for this is on p. 117.

14. For the last trick you will need a rubber band. Stretch it over your little finger, across the back of your hand, and hook the end over your thumb below the joint. Pull the double strands behind the last set of knuckles. The band should feel tight. Bet you can't take off the rubber band without using your other hand! You may not shake it off or rub your hand against anything, either. That's

considered cheating. Of the 200 people we tried this stunt on, only one could do it. She was double-jointed.

ANSWERS

1. The correct way to write the number is 12,111.
   Eleven thousand is 11,000
   Add eleven hundred 1,100
   and add eleven 11
   _____
   12,111

2. The number of dots is forty-five.

3. You must wrap the string between two and three times around your head to equal your height. Children sometimes have a larger head in relation to their height and the wraps are close to two full turns. Surprisingly, the ratio of head wraps to height is pretty much the same for short, fat people, tall, thin ones, and most in betweens.

4. Dry sand weighs more than wet sand. Water surrounding the sand takes up space. Since water weighs less than sand, the dry litre weighs more. Test this by wetting a pile of sand. Scoop up a litre of the wet sand and compare it with a litre of dry sand. Do not fill the litre with dry sand and then pour in the water.

5. The litre of milk weighs more than the litre of cream. Cream will float on top of milk, so you

know it ought to weigh less. But it seems as if it should weigh more because it feels thicker.

6. The cork ball would weigh about half a tonne. A 1.5-metre ball would be about 453 kilogrammes, but it would still float! A 1.5-metre ball of water weighs four times as much, about 1814 kilogrammes. The cork would displace much less than its weight in water and so it would float.

7. The answer to the mysterious sequence is: O, T, T, F, F, S, S, E, N, T.
   If you still need more help: one, two, three, four, five, six, seven, eight, nine, ten.

13. You can't swing a pendulum so that it hits the bottle on the return trip unless it hits the bottle on the way out. The path of a pendulum swing is an ellipse. If the ball swings to one side of the target on the way out, it will miss the target by the same distance on the other side on the return trip.
   Carnival people used this as a con. They would twist the string so that the ball would be spinning. A spinning ball takes a different path than one thrown flat. With practice, you can put enough spin on the ball so that the ellipse is flattened and the bottle is knocked over as the pendulum returns to its starting place.

INDEX